ARE YOU OFEENDED YET?

YOU'LL SOON BE ENCOURAGED.

For Encouragement

By Mary L Lumsden
Inspirational Poems
It Only Takes a Little Belief

Copyright © 2024 by Mary L Lumsden
Published in the United States of America
ISBN Paperback: 978-1-963917-49-9
ISBN Hardback: 978-1-963917-50-5
ISBN eBook: 978-1-963917-51-2
Library of Congress Control Number: 2024918365

All rights reserved. No part of this publication may be reproduced, stored in a retrieval system or transmitted in any way by any means, electronic, mechanical, photocopy, recording or otherwise without the prior permission of the author except as provided by USA copyright law.

INTRODUCTION

The Old Testament scriptures are there to remind us not to follow the ways of our ancestors before us, but to follow Jesus's way of life to salvation.

- Jn. 3:16-17, Jn. 14:6, Rom. 12:1-2, Jn. 14:12-14

BE BLESSED:

PLEASE FOCUS ON THE SCRIPTURES. GOD'S WORDS ARE MORE POWERFUL & STRONGER THAN MINE.
I'M JUST HERE TO POINT YOU TO THINKING ON HIS WORDS.

ISAIAH 55: 8-9

ISA. 55:8- for my thoughts are not your thoughts, neither are your ways my ways faith the LORD.
ISA. 55:9- For as the heavens are higher than the earth, so are my ways higher than your ways, And my thoughts than your thoughts.

BE BLESSED
IN JESUS NAME

INSPIRATIONAL POEMS

TOPICS:

1. LISTEN
2. SELFISHNESS
3. WARNINGS
4. PAY ATTENTION
5. FOCUS
6. BE GRATEFUL
7. JUST DO IT

LISTEN

YOU MUST BELIEVE

Believe that God shed his grace

So that you may develop faith

Without God's grace

There can be no faith

Because you must believe that Jesus is the way.

-Acts 18: 24-27, Romans 3: 22-26, Romans 10:13-17

JESUS WILL FIX IT

This is what He's saying, let it go and let it be.

I'll fix it in a minute or after a while

I see it because you're my child.

When you call on me

There's nothing I don't see

That is why I say let it go and let it be.

This is why I want you to call on me

I can fix it, you see! Just, call on me.

−Ex. 14:13-14, Psa. 34:17, Prov. 16:3-5,
1Pet. 5:7, Jer. 29:11, Psa. 46:10-11

YOU'VE TRAINED THE FLESH, NOW IT'S TIME TO TAME THE FLESH

We gave the flesh its way.

Now it's time for us to say.

Flesh! This Day!

I'm going to do it God's way.

So, old desires!

I'm not for hire.

I am on fire for the Lord's desire.

So get the devil off the wire.

Let him know you're not for hire.

-Gal. 5:16-26, Rom. 8:13, Col. 3:5-7, Rom. 6:5-6, Rom. 12:1 -2,Rom. 8:5-8, Gal. 6:7-8, 1 Cor. 9:27, Rom. 13:14, Mat. 26:41, Jam. 1:14-22

CHOSEN THEN FROZEN

You! where chosen.
So why are you standing there frozen?
Frozen in time that really blows my mind.
Time is still moving!
Why are you standing awing and owing?
Don't you know it's time to keep moving?
Move toward God so he can use you his way.
Don't you know the devil wants to snatch you this day! *- Jn. 10:10, 25-30*
These days are getting crazier and wild.
Can't you see this is the enemy's style?
Styling and profiling for everyone to see
And he looks and says another target for me. He knows you were chosen.
So, he throws out those distractions,
Just to see your reactions.
Now, you're frozen, when you know you were chosen.
JESUS was chosen not frozen. He kept on moving.
- Exo.19: 3-5, Jn. 15:16-17, Lk. 9:34-36

MAGNIFY GOD STOP MAGNIFYING THE MESS

Magnify God stop magnifying the mess
Magnify God you won't have time to stress
Can't you see that it's only a test?
Can't you see the devil's is trying to keep
you in the mess.
Don't let the stress of the mess stop you from
passing your test.
Just give God all of the mess.
Then see how good it feels when you're at rest
AND STOP MAGNIFYING ALL THAT
MESS.

-Mat. 15:1-11, Jer.29:11-13, Psa. 19:1-14,Psa. 91:14-16, Phil. 4:6-7, Psa. 55:1-5, 22-23, Isa. 26:3-5

EVERYONE HAS A PAST

Everyone has a past
And it has passed and time moves on.
The thing to do is to leave it alone
Time wasn't meant to stand still
It is a rolling wheel
And it keeps rolling on
until the past has gone.
Keep moving like that wheel
And don't stand still.
You don't want to live in the past all alone
So trust God he will help us to move on.

- Prov. 3:5-6, Jer. 29:11
Isa. 43:18-19, 25-26, 2 Cor. 5:17-18

READ IT, RECEIVE IT, BELIEVE IT, TRUST IT

When you read it

You must receive it

In order to believe it

You must trust it or

It's a waste of time to even touch it

Handle it with care and it will get you there

Where you need to be

Because salvation is free

Free for you and for me

- Josh. 1:8, Lk. 24:44-49, 1 Thes. 2:13,
Prov. 3:5-6, Jn. 3:16-18

I AM NOT/BUT I AM

I AM not a mess maker
I AM a mess breaker
I AM not a stress maker
I AM a rest maker
I AM not a taker
I AM the maker
I AM not a risk taker
I AM the regulator
I AM not the problem
I AM the problem fader (**JESUS**)

- Jer. 29:11-13, 2 Cor. 1: 21-22, Jn. 3: 16-18, Jn. 8:58
Jn. 6:35, Jn. 8:12, Jn. 10: 9,11,14, Jn. 11:25, Jn. 14:6, Jn. 15:1

SEX IS NOT FOR RECREATION

Sex is not for recreation - *1 Cor. 7:1-9*

But was created by God for procreation - *Gen. 4:1-2*

For a husband and wife to come together - *Gen. 9:7-12, Psa. 128:1-3*

And bring forth life which is God's creations - *Gen. 4:25-26*

And to bring forth nations - *Gen. 12:1-3*

We must teach this generation - *1 Cor. 6:13-20*

That sex is not a recreation - *2 Cor. 7:1-2*

But was created to continue generations

That produces many nations

To birth God's creations

But yet it shows we need salvation. - *Rom. 10:9-11, Jn. 3:16-19*

In order to sustain from fornication. - *1 Thes. 4:1-8*

WHAT IS THIS THAT I HEAR

What is this that I hear
That you don't want to come near.
Near enough to hear what have I to say.
Say about your ways
On what is causing you to stray
Stray from my words
And you know you've heard.
You know you can't say
You never heard of me on this day.
My name is JESUS, I know everything I say is right.
Can't you see that's why the world is in such a fight?
Fighting for their rights day and night.
When I am the way, the truth and the life.
Only, what I say is right! 2 Chron. 7:14-18, Mat. 13:13-16
- Jer. 6: 10,19, Isa. 42:20, Jer. 11:10, Jer. 25:4-7

LET GO OF THINGS OF THE PAST ONLY WHAT GOD SAYS WILL LAST

It doesn't matter what people say - *2 Cor. 5:17-18*
Because Jesus is the only way
They laugh, they joke, they may even take a smoke
But one thing I know; He's no joke.
Whatever God says comes the past. - *Mat. 24:32-35*
That's how I know his word will last.
Stop listening to what people say.
Your past it wasn't meant to stay.
It was just a lesson to keep you here
Just for this day. (Testify)!
- Isa. 55:11, Isa. 43:18-19, Acts 2:38, Jn. 14:6-10,
Phil. 3:13, Jer. 29:11, Mat. 6:33, Jer 33:3

TRUST LONGER IT'S HARD, BUT JESUS ALWAYS COME THRU

We do this and we do that
Trying to wear all of these hats.
Sit down and take off those hats
Jesus never told you to do this and do that.
He said trust me I've done all of this and all of that
There's no need for all of those hats.
Trust me I can do all this and all that
Without wearing all of those hats.

- Prov. 3:5-7, Isa. 46:10-11, Jer. 17:7-8, Isa. 40:30-31, Ps. 25:1, Mat. 6:25,27, Rom.8:28, Phil.4: 6-7, Mat. 19:26

STOP CATCHING EVERYTHING THE DEVIL THROW AT YOU

When he throws anger -*Psa. 37:8, Prov. 15:1-2*
You catch a smile
When he throws bitterness -*Rom. 12:17-19*
You know he's foul
When he throws envy -*Jam.3:14-17, 1 Cor.13:4*
Rebuke him he's your enemy
When he throws jealousy -*Jam. 3:16, Titus 3:3, 1 Tim. 6:4*
Just let him be because
misery is his company.
Well, that is just not you and me
So stop catching everything the devil
throw at you, you see! In Jesus name.

- Isa. 26:3, 12, Jam. 4: 1-8, Jn. 10:10, 1 Pet. 5:5-9

CAN'T ESCAPE REALITY

You can't escape reality going into fantasy
reality will still be there when you come back
from wonderland.
You wonder and you ponder
But you come up with no solution.
That's because we too come to the conclusion
that, our Lord Jesus Christ is the solution.
He is not an illusion HE is the only conclusion.
Reality check! JESUS IS THE ANSWER.

- 1 Cor. 2:14, Heb. 4: 12-13, Phil. 4: 8-9,
Rom. 1: 19-20, Titus 2:11-14, 1 Pet.2:9,
Mt. 11: 28 30, Jn. 14: 6-7, Mk. 9:23-24

DOUBLE EXPOSURE, AND, IT'S ALREADY BEEN EXPOUND

When he throws anger *-Psa. 37:8, Prov. 15:1-2*
You might have been exposed
And you've already been told *- 1 Thes. 5:27*
Told that you've been made whole *- 1 Thes. 5:23-24*
So hold on to God's unchanging hand *- Heb. 13:8-9*
The devil can touch you but you can stand *- Job 1-42*
Stand for the Lord Jesus Christ *- Jam. 1: 6-8*
The only one who can hold your life
-Deut. 30:19-20, Heb.4:12-13
The life that God gave you *-Jn. 3:16-17*
And He said, He will never leave or forsake you
-Deut. 31:8
So devil keep your hands in your pockets
Because you're leaving here like a rocket *-Rev. 20:1-3*
Don't get it twisted *- 1 Jn. 3: 7,9*
I don't want you to miss it *-1 Jn. 3:4*
Your rocket is going down not up *-1 Jn. 3:8, Rev. 20:10*
You're about to get a taste of your own cup.
In Jesus name. Amen

NOT A THREAT BUT AN ASSET

You helped me to get courage -*Psa. 55:22, Isa. 41:10-13, Deut. 31:6*

Because God said don't worry -*Jer. 17:7-8, Lk. 12:25, Mt. 6:34*

I got your back when that old devil attacks - *Acts 9:1-6*

He's creeping around, and he's still on the grounds -*Psa. 23:4*

But there's no reason for you to frown. -*Psa. 27:1*

Thank you devil for your attacks -*Rom. 8:31, Psa. 27:2-3*

Because I know who's got my back - *Psa. 27:5*

Jesus is the one who will take all my slack

So if you think you're a threat you're way off track

Because know God's got my back -*Deut. 31:7-8*

And you merely an asset trying to be a threat

The more you attack the stronger I get. -*Exod.-15:2-3*

In Jesus Name

YOU! CAN'T CONTROL TIME, GOD DID IT ALL

You can't control the time
It's not yours and it's not mine
The time belongs to God he will control it,
any way he please.
He can move it fast or he can move it slow.
Just don't go ahead of him, I'm sure he will let you know.

- Gen. 1:14-15, Gen. 8:21,22, Psa. 104, Psa. 31:14-15,
Ecc. 3:1-11, Acts 1:6-9, 1 Thes. 5:1-11,
Prov. 16: 4, 7, 9, Prov. 21:5

UNTIL!

Until you seek me! I am going to just look at you.
Until you call on me I won't come to you.
Even if you don't seek me I will always see you.
Until you ask me, what shall I do?
Until you call on me, I will not answer you.

God is waiting for your call. So UNTIL!

*−Isa. 55:3-7, Jam. 4: 8-10, Jer. 29: 11-14, Mat. 6:31-34, Mat. 7:7
Isa. 1:15-20, 2 Chron. 7: 14*

STOP GOING TO YOUR DESERT, THERE'S NOTHING THERE

Stop going to your desert there's nothing there

Not even the tumbleweeds are going anywhere

They blow here and they blow there.

But, they really aren't going anywhere.

That's how it is if you just don't care.

But God cares if you go here or there.

He wants to take you everywhere.

Places you thought you'd never go.

That is because He loves you so.

God will show you what you really don't know,

So always let him show how much he loves you so.

Don't be a tumbleweed toss to and fro.

Find out what God wants you to know.

And he will take you as far as you want to go.

- Phil. 3:12-14, Lk. 9:57-62, Phil. 4:13, Jer. 29:11, Jer. 33:3

SELFISHNESS

LOOK WHERE THAT LETTER "I" IS RIGHT IN THE MIDDLE OF THE WORD "SIN"

Get yourself out of the way "I" won't win

"I" keeps you anx "I"ous, there's that "I" again

Right in the middle, it just has to get in.

It's not about us, but, the one who brought us in.

Jesus is the one who helps us see our sins.

"I" will go nowhere, we need Jesus

who brought us in. *-Jn. 15:4-7*

Not "I" who is full of "Sin". *-1 Cor. 6:19-20, 1 Cor. 7:22-23, 1 Pet. 2:7-9, Rom 3:23-26*

-Rom. 8:5-8, Prov. 3:5-6, Psa. 46:10, Isa. 42:8

ARE YOU OVER YOURSELF YET?

Get Over Yourself, Get Self Out The Way,
Wrong Thinking! Check Your AAR
(Attitude, Actions and Reactions).
The D's In Your Life Are Showing,
(Denial, Danger, Destruction).
You're Not depending.
I AM God, I AM The Focus,
Get Your Mind Off The Matter.
Jesus Is On His Way Back.
Read it. Control Your Emotions!
Check yourself! What is this I hear?
People's Advice! Bad advice. Believe God!
Come Out Of The World.
Give It To GOD.
God is Not The Author Of Confusion.
He Is The Solution.

-Jer. 29:11-13 Isa. 43: 18-19

DON'T PUT "I" BEFORE ASKING

When "I" comes before asking
You're still in your will
"I" will seal the deal
When "I" comes before asking
I don't think you're the master
When "I" comes before asking
Can't you see you're heading for disaster?
Ask in Jesus name then your "I's" will
ask for the "Lord's Will". - *Isa. 55:11*

-*Isa. 55:6-9, Jam, 4:13-16, 1Thes. 5:17-18, Prov. 3:5-6*

THE MAN THAT THINKS ONLY OF HIMSELF

The man that thinks only of himself
He will be left by himself
To himself
With himself
Because he is all about himself. (get over yourself)
The selfie is about Jesus. *- Jn.3:16-18, Jn. 10:10-11*

-Isa. 66:1-4, Rom. 12:3-5, Rom. 12:9-16, Prov. 11:29-30

THE "I" "SIN" DROME

Get the "I"s out of your mouth

And put your "eyes" on the Lord Jesus Christ

The "I"s can get you in trouble

But the "eyes" will help you see God. - *Psa. 121: 1-8, Psa.*

119:1-16

-2 Tim. 3:1-5 Isa. 14:12-15

LOOK OUT FOR MR. "I" AND MR. "LET'S" AND THEIR COUSIN "SELFISHNESS"

I want to go here and want to go there
Now let's go here and let's go there
Oh! You, you'll get there
Now I need to go here, now let's go there
Oh! You don't need to go anywhere
Well, how about this I don't care if you don't get to go anywhere.
Let selfishness take you there. *-Phil. 2:1,5*

-Phil. 2: 3-4, 2 Tim. 3:2-5, 1 Jn. 3:17-18, Phil. 2:21, Jam. 3:16-17 Rom. 15:1-3, Rom. 2:8-11

WARNINGS

THE ATTACK

We were expecting another 911 attack
But Oh my goodness! look what has come back
We have a COVID-19 ATTACK.
We can't see it
But it is oh so near
And it's taking our loved ones that are oh so dear.
You can see how everyone is in so much fear.
We can't fight it, but I know who can.
Give it to the invisible God, the Lord Jesus Christ.
The one that said I hold your life.- *(Jerh. 1:5 NLT, Isa. 54:16-17)*.
As soon as we pray and give no slack.- *(1 Thes. 5:17-18)*.
We know that this COVID-19 will have to turn back.
God is not a man that he should lie.- *(Num. 23:19, Isa. 55:11)*.
So if we don't truly repent we will surely die.-*(Ezk. 18:20,*

2 Chron. 7:14, Rom. 3:23-24).

-2 Tim. 3:1-5 Isa. 14:12-15

SPEAK!

Don't be afraid to speak boldly
- Acts 28:30-31, Eph.3:10-16, Heb.13:6

About the LORD JESUS CHRIST.

He is the one who saved your life. *- John 10:10*

Cry loud and spare not

While the iron is still hot. *- Isaiah 55:6-9*

And be sure to get saved this day *- John.3: 16-17*

Because JESUS CHRIST is on his way.

So cry loud and spare not.

This may be your last shot. *-Matthew 24:36-39, 42,44*

SPEAK!

HARD HEAD-HARD HEART

Renew that mind God will change your heart

This is how it all starts.

We know who's putting it in our head.

Sounds like what the devil said.

Why are you listening to that mess?

It's only causing you to stress.

And definitely not be blessed.

Renew your mind and not harden your heart.

Then Jesus can give you a brand new start. *Rom.12:2*
2 Cor. 5:17, 6:1-2

-Isa.6: 8-10, Jer. 16:12-15, Jer. 18:9-12, Rom. 2:5, Acts 28:27

WHY ARE WE SO HARD TO CONVINCE

Oh Lord, why are we so hard to convince?
Running around as if we have no sense.
When your word has already made a lot of sense.
These are your words that we've already heard.
Why aren't we putting them into action?
To show that you're the coming attraction.
Well! I guess your actions will have to
speak louder than your words.
Because they're acting as if they never heard.
Heard in your word, you're coming back.
I think we should get back on track.
Tracking down your word and
believing what we've heard.
Now that you got our attention and
your words are making sense.
I believe you have somebody convinced.

-1 King 18: 20-39, Jer. 6: 10, Jer. 35: 15, Ezek. 2:4-10, Mt. 13:

THINK BEFORE YOU SPEAK, THEN PRACTICE WHAT YOU PREACH

Renew that mind God will change your heart
This is how it all starts.
We know who's putting it in our head.
Sounds like what the devil said.
Why are you listening to that mess?
It's only causing you to stress.
And definitely not be blessed.
Renew your mind and not harden your heart.
Then Jesus can give you a brand new start. - *Rom.12:2*

2 Cor. 5:17, 6:1-2

-Rom. 12:2-3, Phil. 2:3-4, Mat. 23:15-16, Lk. 16:13-15, Mk 7:5-7, Lk. 20: 46-47,

WHAT'S WITH THIS MURDER, KILLING, SHOOTING AND STEALING?

What's with this murder, killing, shooting and stealing? -*Jhn.10: 10-18*

Don't you see this is what the devil is revealing?

Anger, frustration, bitterness, and strife.

All the things that shouldn't be a part of our life.

But sense Jesus had to go through these things.

Now we see what this world has to bring.-*1 Jn. 3:8, 1Pet.1:14-16*

Now we understand why He said follow me.-*Jn. 10:27-30*

He will protect us as you can see. -*Jer. 33:3-9*

Remember all you need to do is to follow me. *Jn. 8:12*

WHAT LIE HAVE YOU STOLE OR WHAT LIE HAVE YOU TOLD
(Brought up) (Made up)

What lie have you heard somebody say,
That things are suppose to be that way.
What lie have you made up and dressed it up?
Stop dressing up those lies.
It's just a matter of pride.
Just tell the truth.
God knows every step we take.
And every move we make.
Even when we sleep we're not that deep.
So get rid of the lies and tell the truth.
Then everything God says will take root. *Jn. 8:26-32*

-Gen. 27: 19-24 Lk. 22: 54-62, Gen. 20: 1-14

STANDING AND FREEZING FOR NO GOOD REASON

Why are you standing there freezing for no good reason
Don't you know the time of the season?
But you're standing there freezing for no good reason
All the devil sees is you're standing there teasing
Gives him a reason to test your teasing
So don't temp the devil for no good reasons
Just think of pleasing the God of all seasons.
(Let Jesus Be Your Cover)

*-1 Cor. 6: 12-20, Prov. 3: 5-6, Gal. 5: 17-21,
Heb. 13:4-5, Jer. 29:11*

PAY ATTENTION

MOMS VS. KIDS

Being a mom can be fun
Sometimes they make you feel so dumb
When the kids are smarter than you
You have to figure out what you're going to do
You go back to school to sharpen you tools
And come back with some more rules
Oh well that didn't do
These kids now, are still smarter than you.
Solution, stay in the word of God
And you will get smarter too.

-Prov. 4:7

SHUT OFF "YOUR" THOUGHTS

Shut down - Be still *-Psa. 46:10-11, Exod. 14:14, Psa. 37:7*

Be quiet-Listen *-Isa. 55:8-11, Psa. 32:8-11, Prov. 1:5-7*

Shut away-God and you *-Isa. 1:18-20, Jam. 4:8, 1 Jn. 5:1-5*

Shut out-All nonsense *-Prov. 3:1-13, Prov. 4:1-7, Prov. 5:1-6*

BEING OBEDIENT PLEASES GOD

Do what I say -*Jn. 15:16-17*

I'll do what you ask - *Mt. 7:7-8, 21-27*

Do what I say not for self-gain -*Phil. 2:3-5*

But do it that your fruit will remain -*Isa 55:8-11,13,Jn.15:1-8,16*

Do what I say if you want to see change -*Isa 43:18-19, Rom.12:1-2*

Do what I say and nothing will be the same. - *1 Sam. 15:22-25, Jn. 14:15-16, Col. 3:20*

Phil. 4: 14-19

THE TEST

Everything looks a mess *-1 Thes. 5:9, 19-24*
But it is only a test *-Romans 12:2-3*
And in the end we will be blessed *-1 Peter 4:12-14*
Keep Jesus the focus in the mess *-Psalm 28:7*
Only then you won't get stressed *-James 1:2-4*
Don't get focused on the mess *-Psalm 26:2-3*
Just say to yourself it's only a test *-Hebrews 12:10-11*

And Jesus will bring us through this mess.

GOD IS NOT THE DEATH ANGEL WE JUST TURNED A DEAF EAR

Why is it that you don't want to hear?
Hear the truth there's so much proof.
Proof that he chose you and will show you what to do.
Why are you turning a deaf ear.
Pretending like you don't hear.
When this is the time to draw near.
So you can hear with both ears.
Hear what God has to say.
There's no time left to play.
He's trying to tell us he is the only way
To salvation today *-Jn. 14:6, Jn. 3:16*

-Jn. 10:10-14, Isa. 53:1, 6-8, Mat. 11:11-15, Ex. 15:23-26,
Jer. 11:6-8, Isa. 51:4-7, Heb. 3:5-19

THE FIGHT IS ALREADY FIXED

(HE'S GOT THIS)

Who told you, you have to fight as if you have the might.
Who told you, you could win without Him.
Did you win over sin?
Since the beginning of time it has already been fixed.
Because God was always in the mix.
That's why he sent Jesus to the cross.
He is the one God made the boss.
So you see the fight was already fixed.
Thank God we don't have to get in the mix.
We just have to pray and repent.
Yes, Jesus was already sent.

-Prov. 3:5-6, 2 Chron. 7:14, Rom. 12:19, 2 Chron. 20:17

DON'T TRY TO GET ATTENTION TRY TO PAY ATTENTION

Pay attention to who and what's in front of you.
- Prov. 16:20- 30, Mat. 23:1-39

Don't let everything astound you. *- Gal. 6:7-9*

Don't look for attention. *Prov. 3:5-6*

He is the attention grabber.*-Psa. 123: 1-4*

Look at Nimrod's people they are a perfect example.
- Gen. 11:1-9

Seek too much attention he will make you babble.

So give God's only son the attention. *- Isa. 51:7-8*

Yes, Jesus he's the only one that's worth mentioning.

And the only one that should get all of our attention.
- Lk. 9:32- 35

THE WORLD IS IN GREED AND IN NEED

The world is in greed - *Lk. 12: 15-18,*

1 Cor. 6: 9-10, Mt. 6:33

But yet the greed is not satisfying their need - *Lk. 12:16-21*

They are in need of a Savior - *Jn. 3:16-17 8-13*

To show them some favor - *Isa. 58:11, Prov. 18:22, Psa. 5:12,*

Psa. 84:11-12

To save them from their sins - *Eph. 2: 8-10, 2 Cor. 5:21,*

Rom. 10:9-10

That will put them on the mend - *Hosea 6: 1-3, Jer. 30:17-18*

God only wants to show us how to win - *Rom. 6: 11-14,*

Rom. 8:8-13

And learn how to stop giving into sin. -*Col. 3:5* (Obey

God) -*Ex. 19:5-6, Rom. 2:5-13*

THE PLAN

JESUS, JESUS the CHRIST
Oh how good and Oh how nice
To know you hold our life.
Our life is in your hands
And so, I think I understand.
Because you know well who I am
And you alone have the plan.
A plan for every life
Through all the strife.
Strife was a part of your life!
So when you died and rose again
That was the ultimate plan.
To show us that, it wasn't the end.

-Jer. 29: 11-13 Jn. 3:16-17

YOU CAN'T LISTEN WITH YOUR EYES YOU HAVE TO LISTEN AND HEAR WITH YOUR EARS

(REBELLIOUS)

Don't listen with your eyes

It's not very wise

But listen and hear with your ears

It may stop some of your fears

You can't listen with your eyes

Then you can't see thru the disguise

of the unwise. - *Mk. 4:11-12*

So listen and hear with your ears -*Jer. 5:18-23*

So God can draw you near. - *Jam. 4:7-8*

- 1 Cor. 2:9-10, Mt. 11:1-15, Isa. 28:23,
Prov. 8:32-35, Jer. 7:22-28

FOCUS

I AM GOD, I AM THE FOCUS!

I AM GOD, stop looking at everyone else,
I chose you, it's not about you but all about me.
Put self on the shelf
And put God on the table I AM the one that is able,
Wake up, Pay attention.
Follow the right person, Jesus is love.
What is this that hear!
Get rid of that attitude. I never
Operated on man's time. Let go of the past.
Only what I Say will last.

- Mat. 7:1, Mat. 6:33, Jn. 15:16, Jam. 3:14-15, 2 Tim. 3:1-5
Ecc. 3:1-8, 1 Jn. 2:15, Prov. 16: 1-3

YOU MAY HAVE FEAR, BUT, HAVE FAITH AND FOCUS

You may have fear, but don't be afraid.

But use the faith that I gave.

Now focus on what I've called you to do,

Because this is all about me, and a lot about you.

And, what I want you to do.

The fear will come, need you to faith it out and

focus on who and what it is all about (Me, Jesus).

And try not to have any doubt. (Trust me)!

- Isa. 41:10, Psa. 27:1-3, Lk. 14:27-30, Duet. 6:6-7
Heb. 11:1-3, Heb. 11:6, Prov. 3:5-6, Col.3:2, Jer. 33:1-3

BE GRATEFUL

YOU GOT SAVED, BUT YOU GAVE HIM NO PRAISED

Brave enough to say,
I'll give God all the praise.
For straightening out my story.
So I'll give you the glory.
The glory for cleaning up my mess.
Because all he wants is to do is give us his best.
When you get saved, you know you can rest.
And from now on it's only a test.
A test to see, if you would give him the praise.
After all it was God that gave you the raise.
And I don't just mean money! In Jesus name.

-Psa. 150, Psa. 139:13-14, Jer. 17:14, Psa. 105:1-2, Isa. 12

LORD USE ME

Lord use me

Because all the devil wants to do is accuse me

Lord use me and I won't let the devil confuse me

Lord use me so I can give you the glory,

when I tell your story.

Lord use me to testify,

Not test-a-lie.

Lord use me to give it to them straight.

Ooh... Lord I just can't wait..

But, I will wait for you,

To tell me when and what to do. Lord use me!

- Prov. 3:5-6, Jer. 29:11, Jam. 3:13-18,
1 Pet.5:8-11, Jude 1:9-11, Rev. 12:10-12

CALLED

It is not about what we don't want to do
It's about what God called us to do.
He called us to do his bidding.
Not just sitting
He does the sitting while we do the bidding,
Which to me is so fitting.
You know God sits on the throne
But he's not alone
Jesus sits on his right hand
So he can stand for us again
Oh wow! what a great plan,
For when we fall
He will stand us again nice and tall.

- Exod. 3:1-4,10-12, Jon. 1:1-4, 3:1-4, Acts 9:1-5, Rom. 8:34-39

DON'T LOVE THE MONEY (IT'S JUST A TOOL) MAT. 6:21, 24 GOD CAN TAKE THE MONEY FROM YOU OR TAKE YOU FROM THE MONEY

Why are you so focused on that money?

It seems a little odd.

Don't you know that money truly belongs to God.-*Phil. 4:19, 1 Cor. 10:26*

The bible said he own cattle on a thousand hills. - *Psa. 50:10-11*

Sounds to me that is his will.

He also said the earth is his and the fullness thereof. -

Psa. 24:1

I don't see where he said make money your love.

-- 1 Tim. 6:10

Looks like to me he sent down the spirit descending like a dove.

-Mt. 3:16-17

To rest on the one he loved.

So be careful how you handle his money. It all belongs to him.

He's trusting us to use it wisely or we may be hanging out on a limb. - *Mt. 25:15-29, Lk. 19:2-8, Mt. 6:33-34*

-Acts 5: 1-11, Lk.16:19-31

JESUS PAID THE COST BECAUSE WE WERE LOST

JESUS paid the cost -*Jn. 3:16*

Because we were lost -*Jn. 3:14-15*

Dead in our sins-*Jn. 3:20*

And we wouldn't let him in. -*Jn. 3:11-12, 17*

We closed the door to our hearts - *Heb. 3:8-15*

Simply because we loved the dark. - Jn. 3:19-21

Dark was where we could hide, *Jn. 13:21-30*

And listen to all the devils lies, -*Gen. 3:3-13*

Now that we're in the light. - *1 Pet. 2:9-12*

God just wants us to do what's right. *Jn. 5:33-40*

So Jesus paid the cost on that cross

That we wouldn't have to stay lost. -*Jn. 3:21*

-Psa. 150, Psa. 139:13-14, Jer. 17:14, Psa. 105:1-2, Isa. 12

JUST DO IT

TURN OUR HEARTS BACK TO YOU

Lord turn our hearts back to you
So you, can show us what to do
Lord Jesus you know what to do
Because you are tried and true
You know exactly what to do.
Only you have passed the test
When they nailed you for our mess!
We could have never passed that test.
Three days you said you'd be up and about
It happen three days without a doubt
You rose up and walked out.
So you see it's true
Only you can do what you do
And I know you can definitely show us too.

-Mal. 3:5-7, 2 Chron. 7:14-16, Mt. 13:9, 13-16

JUST TAKE JESUS

It doesn't matter how much money you make
It's Jesus whom you should take
Take Him home when you're all alone
Take Him on when you start to groan
And take Him on when you want to roam
Just take Jesus then you'll see
This is the way it was meant to be

-Phil 4:4-13, 19 Heb. 13:5-6 Psa. 46: 1-7, 10

BETTER TO BE RUDE AND RIGHT THAN TO BE RUDE AND WRONG

-Jn. 8: 1-32, 58-59

They thought Jesus was being rude
When he took them to school.
The school of knowledge
Where there was no college.
They were so amazed at how he taught
That sometimes he had to run out.
But amazingly he didn't get caught.
It was the new way to live which made them so mad.
(truth)
They had the wrong thinking in their heads.
After all they were the ones rude and wrong all the long.
And it took Jesus to come to help them to be strong.
(Believe)
Jesus wasn't rude he was right.

DON'T BE OFFENDED, THE WORD OF GOD IS NOT TO OFFENDED YOU, BUT TO DEFEND YOU AND ME.

-Phil 4:4-13, 19 Heb. 13:5-6 Psa. 46: 1-7, 10

JESUS CAME TO DEFEND, SATAN COMES TO RESENT AND OFFEND.

DON'T BE DISCOURAGED THIS IS FOR ENLIGHTENMENT AND ENCOURAGEMENT
JESUS TRULY IS THE ONLY ANSWER